INSPECTOR SMART

AND THE CASE OF

THE EMPTY TOMB!

CASE FILE

D1630873

BY TIM CHESTER

Inspector Smart and The Case of the Empty Tomb: Case File
© Tim Chester/The Good Book Company, 2014

From an original idea by Michael J Tinker
Inspector Smart © Michael J Tinker 2014

Published by
The Good Book Company Ltd

Tel (UK): 0333 123 0880
International: +44 (0) 208 942 0880
Email: info@thegoodbook.co.uk

Websites:
UK: www.thegoodbook.co.uk
North America: www.thegoodbook.com
Australia: www.thegoodbook.com.au
New Zealand: www.thegoodbook.co.nz

ISBN: 9781909919686

Design and illustration by André Parker
Printed in the UK by CPI Group (UK) Ltd, Croydon, CR0 4YY

Written by Tim Chester

Published by

Author's Note:

Inspector Smart and Chief Inspector
Brown are imaginary characters, but the
people Inspector Smart interviews are
real (though we don't know the names
of the Roman soldiers, so we invented
those). They lived 2000 years ago in the
days of ancient Rome, at the time of
the very first Easter. You can read about
them in the Bible (see page 62).

Some people you will meet in
this book:

Inspector Smart

Born in New Jersey, USA.
Seasoned detective with
the Jerusalem Bureau
of Investigations (JBI).
Reputation for "getting
the job done".

Chief Inspector
Brown

Background: career
policeman in London,
England. Now Smart's
immediate superior at JBI.
Loves coffee, bacon rolls
and his wife, Ethel.

Mary Magdalene

Friendless because of her work – but Jesus showed her compassion and care. She loves to tell people about what has happened to her.

Thomas

Hard-working man who left everything to follow Jesus. Straight talking; not taken in by silly stories. Likes to see proof before he'll believe anything.

Commander Felix

Born in Sicily. Career
soldier; he is deliberate
and careful in all he does.
Prides himself on always
doing his best.

Marcus

Joined the army when he
was 17. Not the brightest
button on a tunic, but
good at what he does –
guarding.

Introduction

"Ah, Inspector Smart. Come in, there's a good chap."

Inspector Smart sat down in front of Chief Inspector Brown's big desk. Brown peered at him from behind a large file.

"You'll enjoy this one. Fascinating. Not your typical case. Usually we have a dead body and have to find the killer. This time we know who the killer is... It's the body we can't find!"

Brown laughed, clearly thinking this was some kind of joke. Smart didn't laugh; he was intrigued. "Tell me more," he said.

"A man called Jesus. About three years ago he started healing people, walking on water, teaching people to love God, welcoming the poor. Standard stuff. Well, except for the healing people. And the walking on water. They were a bit odd.

"Anyway, three days ago the authorities had him executed. Not sure why – I can't find any mention of a crime in the paperwork.

"No matter – the thing is, his body's gone missing. It seems it was put in a tomb and the door was sealed… But now it's gone. I need you to find out what's going on. Ask around. Question a few suspects. The usual sort of thing."

He handed the file to Smart.

"Perhaps it's a conspiracy by his followers," Smart suggested. "But what about the empty tomb? Most likely someone stole the body. Or maybe he didn't really die in the first place."

Brown coughed. "I'd rather you didn't conduct your investigation in my office."

"Sorry," said Smart standing up. "As you say, a bit odd."

Can you help

Inspector Smart solve...

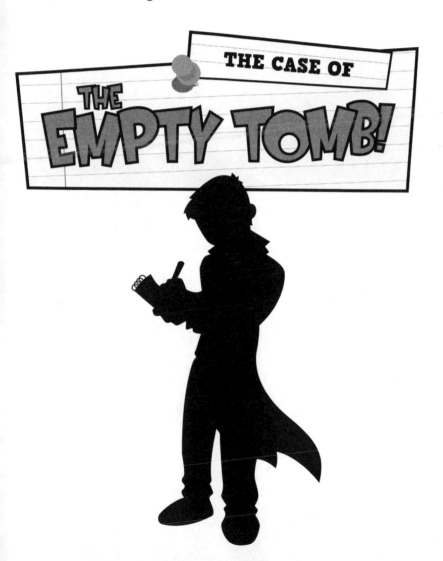

THE CASE OF

THE

EMPTY TOMB!

1

Smart opened the file. At the top was a
newspaper cutting.

The Jerusalem Times

JESUS TO BE CRUCIFIED

Jesus of Nazareth, the preacher and miracle-worker, has been sentenced to death.

He was arrested on Thursday night during a midnight raid in the Garden of Gethsemane. *The Jerusalem Times* understands he was betrayed by Judas Iscariot, one of his own followers. There was a brief struggle, which ended with someone having their ear cut off by a sword. But Jesus healed the ear before he was led away.

Jesus was taken to the house of the High Priest to be judged by the Jewish Council. Various witnesses accused him, but their statements did not agree. Jesus himself said nothing. In the end the High Priest asked him: "Are you the Saviour and the Son of God?" Jesus replied: "I am". This made the Council angry and they decided he was guilty of pretending to be God.

Early in the morning Jesus was taken to Pilate, the Roman Governor. Pilate could find nothing wrong with him, but the crowd called for Jesus to be crucified. So Pilate charged him with being "The King of the Jews". Jesus is expected to be crucified later today.

Jesus is believed to be from Galilee. Everyone has been talking about him since he arrived in Jerusalem last Sunday. During the Passover Festival he has been seen in the temple debating with the religious leaders.

TERRORIST RELEASED

A terrorist and murderer called Barabbas was pardoned today. It is the custom for Roman authorities to release a prisoner as part of the Passover celebrations. This year the crowd was given the option of Jesus or Barabbas. In a surprise choice, they chose Barabbas.

Police are warning people not to approach him.

SPORTS NEWS

Jerusalem FC 0 – 3 Sheffield Utd

Jerusalem FC were beaten by a second-half hat-trick from Sheffield United's star striker, Tim Chester. Full match report on page 8.

Smart thought about it. Barabbas was guilty yet he went free. It looked as if Jesus was innocent yet he was condemned. In a way, Jesus had died in the place of Barabbas. A strange business.

2

Smart turned to the next piece of paper.

Witness Statement:
Commander Felix

Yes, I'd heard about him. He healed the servant of one of my army friends. Jesus just spoke and the illness went away. I'm used to giving commands and people do what I say, but this man could command sickness!

It was my job to crucify him. I didn't like it, but I had my orders. The prisoner is supposed to carry his own cross, but Jesus was too weak. He'd been badly beaten. So we grabbed a stranger from the crowd and made him carry the cross.

It was 9.00am when we nailed him to the cross. Normally people kick and scream, but Jesus was quiet. At one point he said: "Father, forgive them". I've never heard anyone say that before! It gave me a funny turn, I must say. He really seemed to be forgiving me.

Some people were laughing at him. They shouted: "He said he came to save people, but he can't even save himself!" But it seemed to me that Jesus had decided to die.

At noon everything went dark. Very strange – a bit spooky, to be honest. It lasted three hours. Then Jesus shouted: "It is finished". It was as if he had finished what he wanted to do.

It was my job to check he was really dead. He seemed to have stopped breathing, but I pushed my spear into his side. We always do that. If water comes out with the blood, then someone is dead. And water came out of the body of Jesus. Yes, he was definitely dead.

I think he did come to save people. Maybe he was even a King. I know it sounds strange, what with him being dead and everything. But if you'd seen how he died, then you'd know what I mean.

Signed: *Felix*
Name: Commander Felix
Rank: Centurion
Date: Friday

Smart's theory about Jesus not really dying was clearly wrong. Smart had met Commander Felix a few times. He was a tough soldier and not the sort of person to make stuff up. And he'd checked that Jesus was dead.

It was obvious. There must have been some kind of plot to make up a story about Jesus being alive.

3

Witness Statement:

Mary Magdalene

It was early on Sunday morning when I went to the tomb with some other women. We wanted to anoint the body of Jesus with perfume. He'd been so kind to us, and he'd shown us that God forgives everyone who turns to him. We were so upset when he was killed, so looking after his dead body was the least we could do.

We hadn't really thought how we were going to open the tomb, but when we arrived we could see the stone had been rolled away and the tomb was open.

I didn't look in; I was too scared. I ran back to get his followers. I'd rather not give their names – I don't want to get them into trouble. I said: "They have taken Jesus away and we don't know where they've put him".

I came back with them and they went inside the tomb. They were very excited when they came out.

"It's empty," they said. And then they ran off.

I was left standing outside. I didn't know what to do. I just stood there crying. In the end I decided to look inside. I got a big surprise. There were two people in there, shining like angels. Maybe they were angels; I don't know. "Why are you crying?" they asked.

"They've taken Jesus away," I said.

Then I turned round because someone was standing behind me. I thought it was the gardener. He said: "Why are you crying? Who are you are looking for?" I said: "Sir, if you've taken Jesus, tell me where he is and I'll get him".

Then he said: "Mary". I couldn't believe it. I knew right away it was Jesus – but how could it be him? I'd seen him die and now he was talking to me.

I wanted to hug him and never let him go. But he said: "Don't hold on to me because I must

return to my Father. Instead
tell my friends that I'm going to
be with God". So I went to tell
everyone I could think of who
knew Jesus that I'd seen him
alive.

  Then you found me and brought
me in for questioning. That's
what happened. I'm telling the
truth.

Signed: *Mary*
Name: Mary Magdalene
Date: The Sunday after Passover

Can't use this witness

Chief Inspector Brown had written in pen across the bottom, "Can't use this witness". Smart knew why: evidence from a woman wasn't allowed in a court. Smart hated that rule; it didn't seem fair.

But it was true, thought Smart, that her statement wouldn't count. But it did make his theory about a plot unlikely. If you were planning to trick people, then you wouldn't choose a woman as your top witness when people wouldn't take her evidence seriously. Besides, thought Smart, it didn't sound like a story someone would make up.

Smart knew what he wanted to do next. He made a few enquiries and soon he was standing in the barracks talking to a group of soldiers.

4

Police Interview

Marcus, Roman Guard,
Jerusalem Barracks

Smart: So let me get this straight.
You were told to guard the
tomb of Jesus.

Guard: Yes.

Smart: Were you armed?

Guard: Of course.

Smart: A company of armed guards
guarding a dead man?

Guard: Er, yes.

Smart:	And now the body's gone?
Guard:	Er, yes.
Smart:	So what happened?
Guard:	It was stolen.
Smart:	Stolen? You were guarding the tomb and the body was stolen?
Guard:	Er, yes. We fell asleep.
Smart:	All of you?
Guard:	Um, yes.
Smart:	So who stole it?
Guard:	Some of his followers.
Smart:	But his followers are fishermen!
Guard:	Big, strong fishermen!
Smart:	How many?
Guard:	Two.
Smart:	Two fishermen stole the body from armed guards?

Guard:	Actually I think there may have been three of them. Or six. Yes, it was definitely eight.
Smart:	Why?
Guard:	Why were there eight?
Smart:	No, why did they steal the body?
Guard:	Because that's what I was told to say.
Smart:	What did you say?
Guard:	Nothing. I didn't say anything.
Smart:	Who told you to say what?
Guard:	Can't say.
Smart:	Hmm. Well, your commander isn't going to be very pleased when I tell him you let some fishermen steal a body from you.
Guard:	You're going to tell him?
Smart:	Of course.

Guard:	OK, here's the truth. The priests paid us to say the body was stolen. Please don't tell the commander.
Smart:	So what really happened?
Guard:	You won't believe me.
Smart:	Try me.
Guard:	There was an earthquake and an angel...
Smart:	An angel?!
Guard:	I'm not making it up – not this time.
Smart:	An angel came? Then what happened?
Guard:	I don't know. I don't remember. We all kind of fainted. When we woke up the tomb was open and the body was gone. Honestly, that's what happened.
Smart:	Funnily enough, I think I believe you.

Smart's eyes had nearly popped out of his head. An angel?! This case was weird to start with and now it had just got a whole lot weirder. An angel?! Not the sort of thing you'd make up.

Smart wasn't getting very far. He trusted the witness of Mary, but her evidence was not allowed in court. The guards would say the body had been stolen, but Smart knew this was a lie. And no court would believe armed guards had been beaten up by fishermen.

Just then his sergeant came in with a piece of paper.

5

Crime Scene Report

Location: Tomb outside
Jerusalem
belonging to Joseph
of Arimathea

Status: Empty except for
grave clothes

Findings: No signs of a struggle

Hmm, thought Smart. No signs of a struggle. As I suspected. The guard was telling the truth when he said they were lying. Or lying when he said...

Whatever. Clearly the body wasn't stolen. He read on.

Forensic Analysis

Analysis of clothes found at the empty grave of Joseph of Arimathea

Lots of blood. No signs of the body.

Conclusion: The grave clothes have almost certainly been used

to wrap someone who had died
a violent death. The body is now
missing.

Lots of blood →

More blood

"Amazing," said Smart in a sarcastic voice to no one in particular. "I wonder what tests they did to work out there was no body!"

6

A week had gone by without any new leads and Smart was frustrated. What was he going to do next?

He was forming a new theory. Maybe the followers of Jesus had made a big mistake. Maybe they were all just a bit stupid. Maybe they were ready to believe a crazy story. After all, who ever heard of a dead man coming back to life?

Then Smart got lucky. One of his sergeants came running in: "Got a witness for you, sir. Downstairs. Claims he's met this Jesus fellow. You know, the dead one."

Police Interview

Thomas

Smart: I'm told you claim to have seen Jesus.

Thomas: Yes, that's right.

Smart: Recently? Like after he died?

Thomas: Yes. Though he's alive again.

Smart: Tell me what happened.

Thomas:	I was one of his followers, you know. I know him well. Spent the last three years with him. Anyway, last week some of the others told me they'd seen Jesus alive.
Smart:	What did you make of that?
Thomas:	I didn't believe them. It was ridiculous. I mean, who ever heard of a dead man coming back to life?
Smart:	Exactly.
Thomas:	So I told them. I said: "Unless I see the nail marks in his hands and put my finger in his side, I will not believe". I needed evidence. I wasn't going to believe some crazy story.
Smart:	I see your point. So what happened?
Thomas:	Last Sunday we were

together in Jerusalem. The doors were locked and we were all a bit afraid. They'd just killed Jesus and we were worried they might come after us.

Smart: Just tell me what happened.

Thomas: Jesus appeared.

Smart: Really? In a locked room?

Thomas: I'm telling the truth.

Smart: What happened?

Thomas: He said: "Peace be with you". Then he turned to me and said: "See my hands and put your finger in my side. Stop doubting and believe."

Smart: What did you do?

Thomas: What would you do? Only God has the power to make something dead come alive again. So I said to Jesus: "My Lord and my God!"

Thomas clearly wasn't stupid. He wasn't going to believe whatever he was told – he needed evidence. Just like Smart.

Jesus had said: "Stop doubting and believe". Smart thought about all the evidence he'd gathered. He was beginning to believe that Jesus really had come alive again. And Thomas was right – only God has the power to do that.

Thomas has asked him: "What would you do?" Now Smart had to decide. Would he too say to Jesus: "My Lord and my God!"?

Can you help Inspector Smart complete his final report?

Police Report

The Case of the Empty Tomb

On the Friday before the Passover Festival, Jesus was crucified. Three days later the tomb containing his body was found to be empty.

The body was stolen.

Yes ☐   Maybe ☐   No ☐

Jesus didn't really die.

Yes ☐   Maybe ☐   No ☐

His followers were stupid.

Yes ☐ Maybe ☐ No ☐

Jesus came back to life.

Yes ☐ Maybe ☐ No ☐

Signed: Smart

Name: Inspector Smart

7

Chief Inspector Brown read through Smart's report, muttering to himself as he did. "Amazing... Humph... Who'd have guessed?... Amazing."

"Good work, Smart," said the Chief Inspector. "I knew you'd crack it."

"What happens next?" asked Smart.

"Next?" asked Brown surprised.

"If Jesus has come back to life, as he said he would, then everything Jesus said must be true."

"Perhaps," said Brown.

"It means Jesus is our Rescuer – that he died in our place and came back to life so that we can be forgiven."

"Maybe," said Brown.

"And he's Lord, just like Thomas said – my Lord and my God."

"Possibly," said Brown.

"So what happens next?"

"Nothing," said Brown, closing the file.

"Nothing?"

"That's right, nothing. No crime has been committed. The body wasn't stolen. There was no conspiracy. And the last time I checked, coming back to life wasn't a crime. Case closed."

"Nothing!" said Smart to himself as he left the room. "I don't think so. I think everything's changed." And he went to find someone to tell the good news.

Case notes:

Case notes:

Case notes:

Want to read more? These full-colour leaflets will help you to investigate the very first Easter for yourself.

The Easter Mystery

Why was the tomb empty on Easter Sunday? And does it matter?

The Eggcellent Egg Hunt

Crack the eggy puzzles to discover what happened at the very first Easter.

The Great Swap

When Jesus died, an amazing swap took place. But what was swapped? And why?

All of the evidence Inspector Smart investigated comes from the Bible.

Read about the very first Easter and meet some of the people who were there at the time, including Mary Magdalene, the Roman guards and Thomas.

You can read the Bible story for yourself on our special "Smart Sheet", free to download from the websites below.

You'll also find details of the "Inspector Smart and the Empty Tomb" book, and other items in the Inspector Smart range.

www.thegoodbook.co.uk/smart

www.thegoodbook.com/smart
www.thegoodbook.com.au/smart
www.thegoodbook.co.nz/smart